EARLY TO MID-INTERMEDIATE

ALL PRAISE TO THEE

8 HYMN FAVORITES FOR PIANO

BY CAROLYN C. SETLIFF

T0087300

ISBN 978-1-5400-9760-6

EXCLUSIVELY DISTRIBUTED BY

WILLIS MUSIC

HAL•LEONARD®

© 2005 by The Willis Music Co.
International Copyright Secured   All Rights Reserved

Visit Hal Leonard Online at
www.halleonard.com

Contact us:
Hal Leonard
7777 West Bluemound Road
Milwaukee, WI 53213
Email: info@halleonard.com

In Europe, contact:
Hal Leonard Europe Limited
42 Wigmore Street
Marylebone, London, W1U 2RN
Email: info@halleonardeurope.com

In Australia, contact:
Hal Leonard Australia Pty. Ltd.
4 Lentara Court
Cheltenham, Victoria, 3192 Australia
Email: info@halleonard.com.au

O Worship the King

Joseph Martin Kraus
Arr. Carolyn Setliff

Reverently

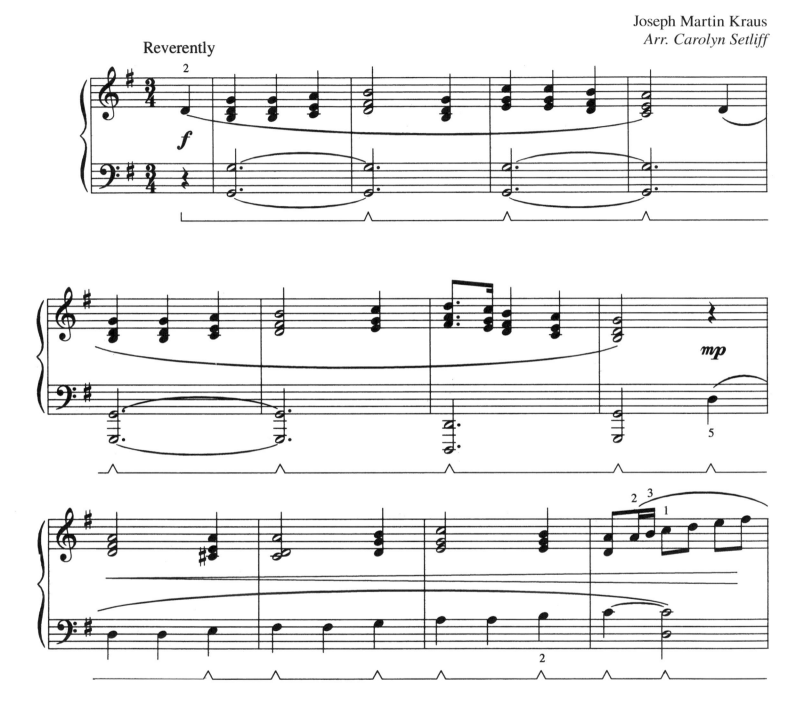

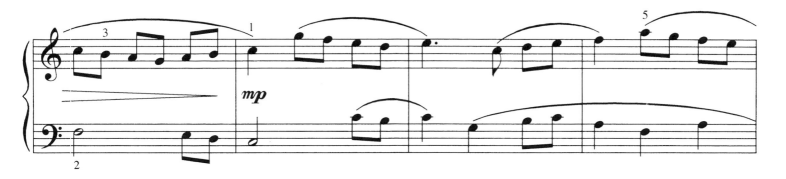

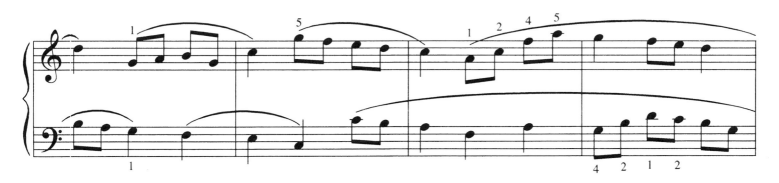

I Sing the Mighty Power of God

Traditional English Melody
Arr. Carolyn C. Setliff

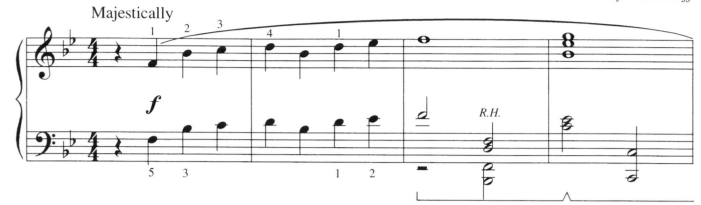

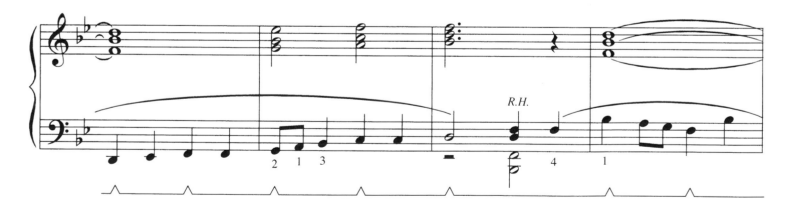

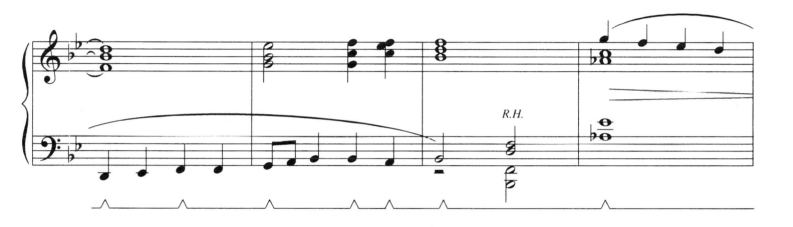

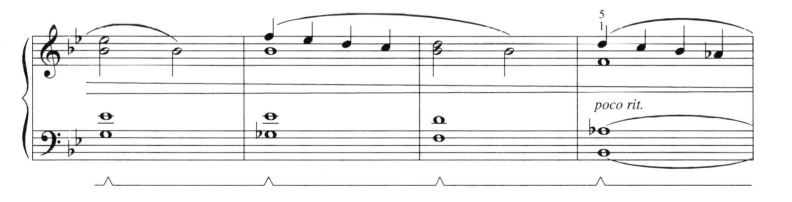

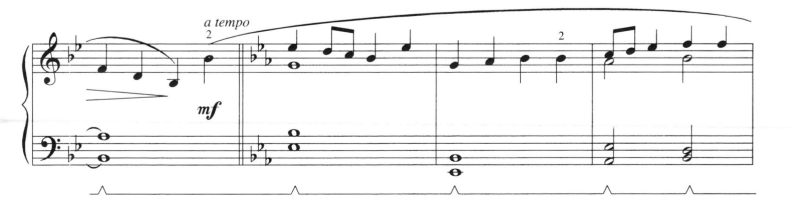

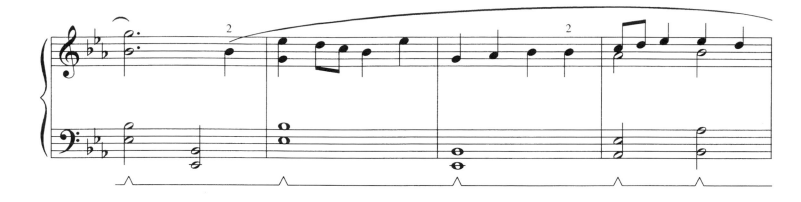

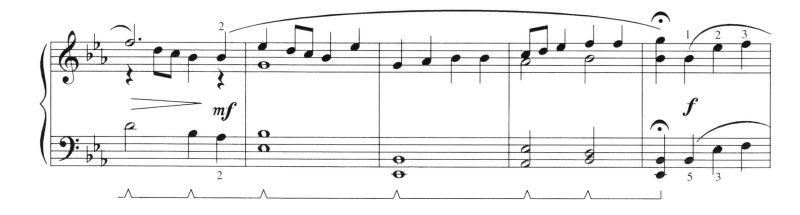

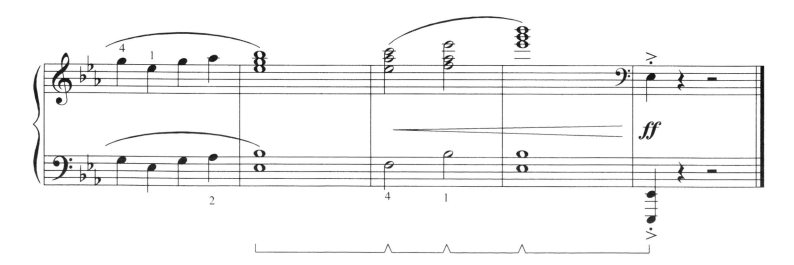

Holy, Holy, Holy

John B. Dykes
Arr. Carolyn C. Setliff

8

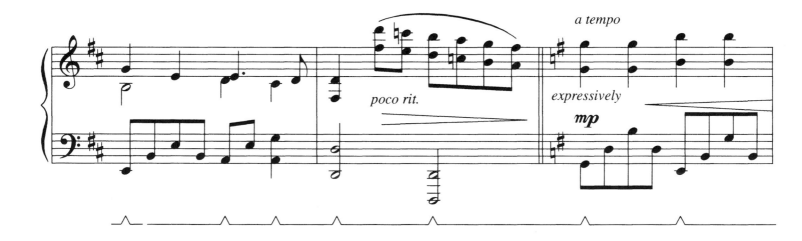

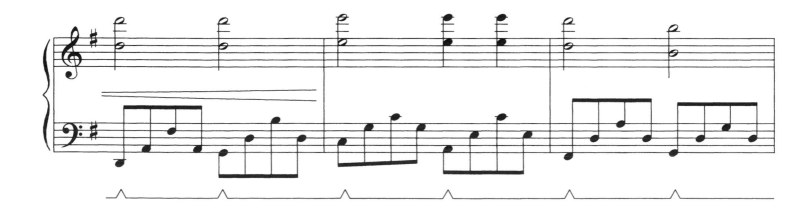

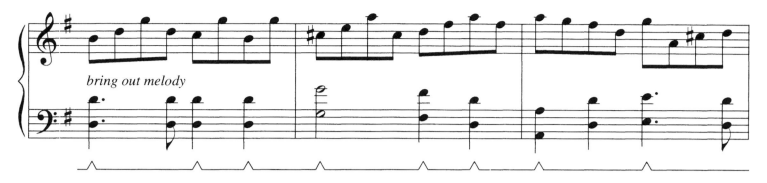

bring out melody

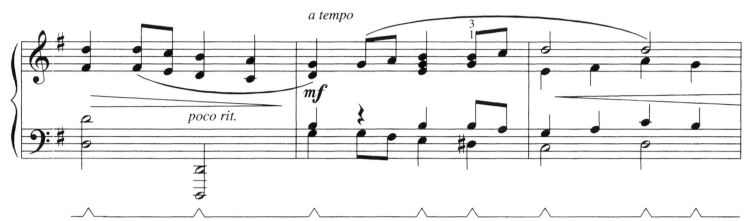

a tempo

poco rit.

mf

f

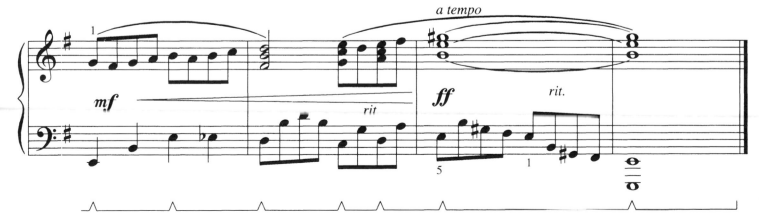

a tempo

mf

rit

ff

rit.

Steal Away

Spiritual
Arr. Carolyn C. Setliff

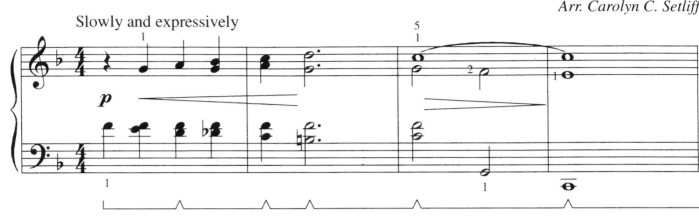

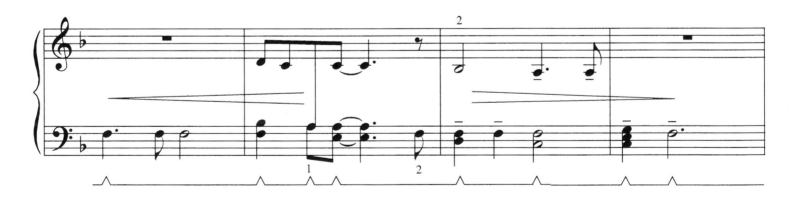

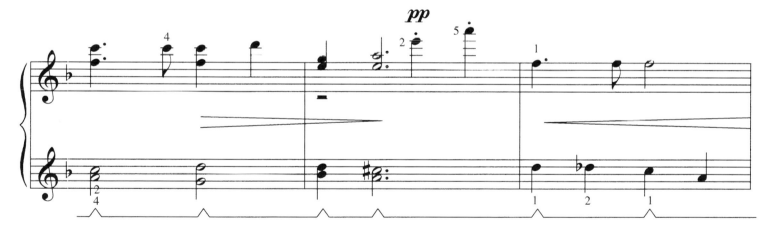

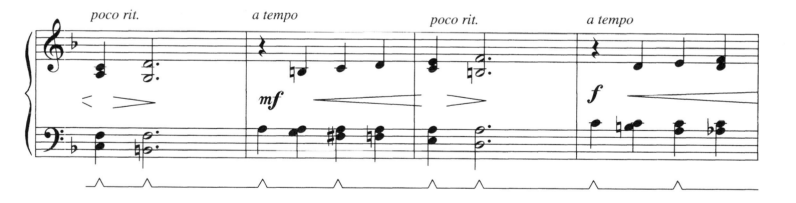

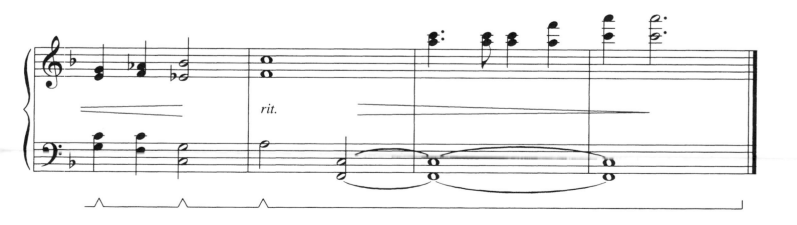

Stand Up, Stand Up for Jesus

George J. Webb
Arr. Carolyn C. Setliff

16

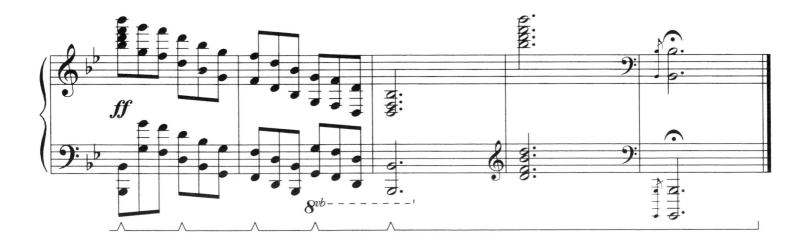

All Praise to Thee,
My God, This Night

Thomas Tallis
Arr. Carolyn C. Setliff

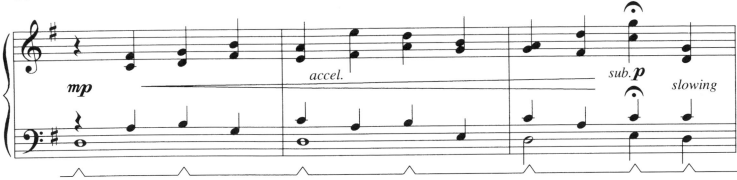

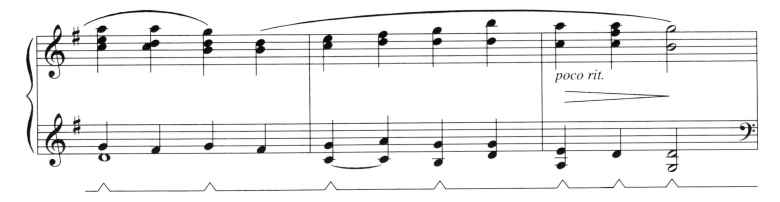

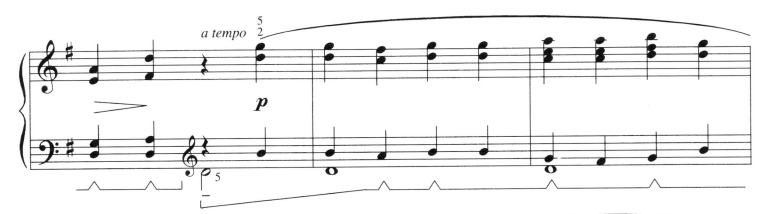

ped. simile

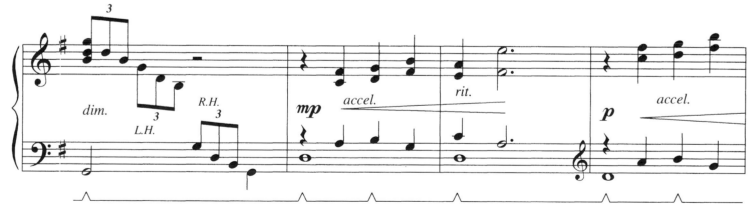

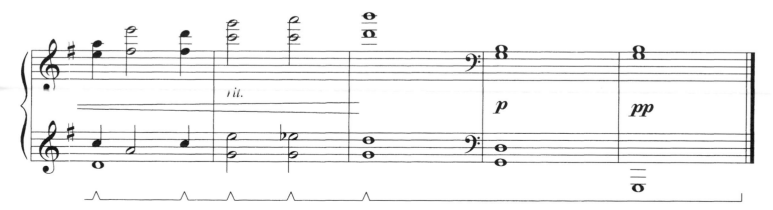

There Is a Balm in Gilead

Spiritual
Arr. Carolyn C. Setliff

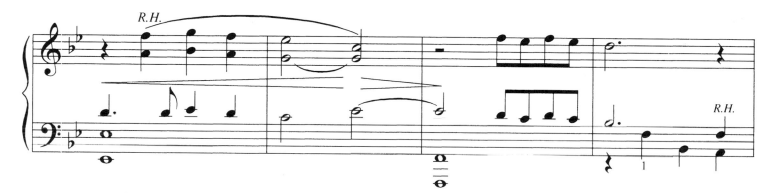

My Country, 'Tis of Thee

Traditional
Arr. Carolyn Setliff

With strong assurance

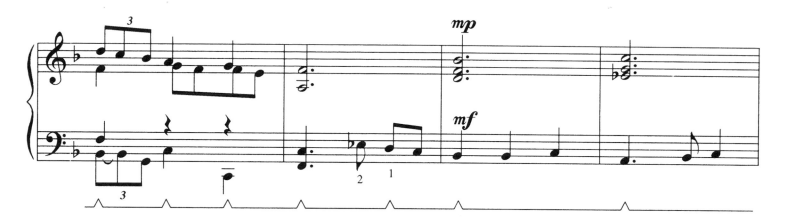

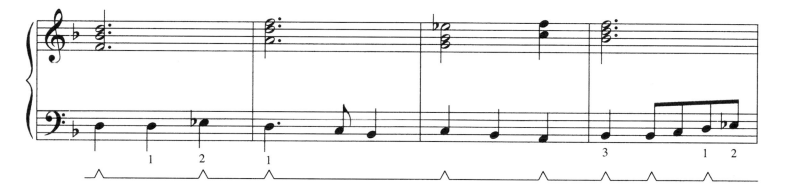

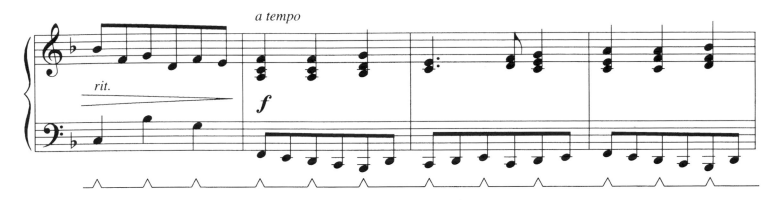

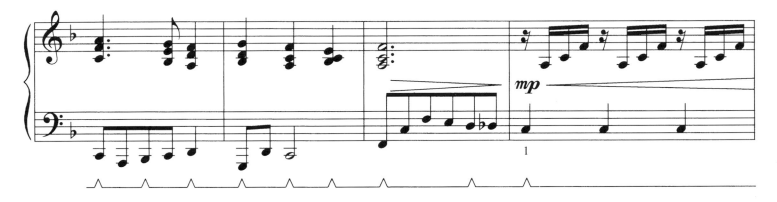